EXPIRED APOLOGIES

SHILPA PANIGRAHI

BlueRose Publishers

First Published in September 2020

ISBN: 978-93-90396-42-9

BLUEROSE PUBLISHERS

www.bluerosepublishers.com

info@bluerosepublishers.com

+91 8882 898 898

Cover Design:

Sanya Rastogi

Typographic Design:

Saurabh Yada

Distributed by: BlueRose, Amazon, Flipkart, Shopclues

DEDICATED TO....

I dedicate this book to my late mother Smt. ***Nirmal Garg*** who was a great Sanskrit scholar and I can never pay off of what best she did for me. And my late father ***Shri Satish Chandra Garg.*** Who served in the Indian armed forces and was my first hero ever.

Dear Rich sky
you have stars in abundance
please return two of mine
my maa and papa

FOREWORD

My past and future selves fell in profound love with each other and delivered some awkwardly sensible poetry to you.

PREFACE

This book is a tool in the hands of those who always wished to peep into the hearts of lovers, since times immemorial.

The book will let you shuffle and explore all the complex and abstract emotions associated with all shades of love.

It will allow you to feel on your skin, both, chills and warmth, in your hearts, tides and tranquility and in your minds, eruptions of epiphanies and emotions.

If only for once, at some point, you feel that you identify yourself in my writing, then I have accomplished my goal as a writer.

I hope you enjoy by feeling the most beautiful emotions of mankind here.

-Shilpa Panigrahi

ACKNOWLEDGEMENT

The verb form of love is known to me because of the man I married. Thank you for being a wonderful husband.

My daughter, who is the most precious blessing in my life and is nothing short of a thesaurus. She is my greatest admirer as well as my best critic. Thankyou Asmi.

My son, an all-rounder. In him, I see the ideal man in the making. He supported me incredibly. Thankyou Arth.

My niece, with her magic wand and cheerful smiles always helping with my coffee curbs as I wrote. Thankyou Manikya.

My sister, my mirror. Who, in fact, has been kind enough to not have killed me for delaying my idea of publishing this book. Thankyou Neha.

TABLE OF CONTENTS

SAME FLAMES

Nothing can extinguish

the fire

in her soul

but another soul

with the same

intense flames

LOVE OBITUARIES

My soul is but a tomb of decaying corpses

always waiting for

the cremating ode

of due apologies

and a few words of love in the obituaries

to find rest and peace

IN YOUR HARBORS

It wouldn't be tiresome

swimming freely in the oceans of your love

but being in your harbors

is also something I look up to

CALL ME THE POLE STAR

It doesn't please me

when you call me

the moon

It reminds me

of it's dark crescent phases

almost like I often tend to have

and ugly cursed scars like

here and there in my heart

those wolves howling at the moon

like my unsatisfied soul

your dedicated yet biased poetry

which I truly am jealous of

and my lonesomeness

which the mighty moon always mocks

It doesn't please me either

when you call me

sunshine

for I'm not sure

for how long

and how many helium fusions

I would have to go through

just to make sure

everyone else is satiating

call me the pole star

I know

I will keep on navigating your soul to mine

making sure we would never get lost

in the crowded world

and even if I ever happen to collapse

I know you would cross your fingers

making wishes about us

RELEASING SINNERS FREE

It is only

when you placed your first kiss

on my neck

all the sinfully dirty thoughts

started taking the shapes

of picturesque art

and all the sinners of this world

started getting credits

of my inappropriate passions

and as I lent

more of my skin to you

to plant a garden

on my body

I also keep declaring

my verdict

by releasing each one of them free

from their sentences

SHE IS LIFE

She is

nowhere between a *maybe* and a *but*

she is

all the cards shown upon the table

front faced

fair and glacé

she is

the trailer

of a rhapsodic extravagant movie

yet to release

she is

a galaxy

unknown

still waiting to be found

perplexed and profound

she is

a bet

won on the last dime

a gold trophy

certified

she is

the colour

most appropriate for the colourblind

she is

the breath

called life

for which

you and I thrive

why wouldn't they hesitate

to look upto her

so enormous

and full

and

whoever dared to walk in

could never wished to seek the way out

CHALLENGE ME

I want more people around me

shaking their heads in disagreement

I DREAM AND BLUSH

This time

it is not the soft blow of wind

who's passionate touch

took control over my ease

and left me urging for more

but him

the way he moved towards me

and kissed me below my ear

whispering words of love

I felt them brushing against my skin

I'm not sure if the wind makes me feel beautiful

or his lips against my skin

I dream and blush

in beautiful hues

A TRANSPARENT HEART

My love was

but an old tarnished antique key

which I had always been ruffling

and cloaking

to access the vault of your heart

which seemed to be publicly available

to all

PAINT ME

Paint me with the colours that talk

and I will sing you like you have already been painted

NO ONE BUT YOU

Not a single

heartbeat

of mine

is ready

to proxy

for someone else

YOU ARE MY POISON

Between death and heartache

She chose him

the perfect amalgam of poisons

I MISS YOU

Your warm breath is the wool

and the deep kisses we shared

are embellishments

on the shawl I knitted for myself

for this world

is too cold

and unworthy

of me

that I miss being in your arms

FIND MY POETRY

If I was illiterate

you would still find poetry

blooming in my garden

some sung in my songs

some flowing through my drapes

and some in just the way

I look at you

LOCK ME

Lock me in a room full of mirrors

I always wished

to be in the most gorgeous crowds

NOISY HEARTBEATS

The oceans

the night sky

all the flowers

and the breeze

pour melodies in my ears

while things with heart beats

just make noise

ALL FLAVOURS OF HER

You will find all flavours in her

she is madness all over

even in her bitterness

she will drive you crazy for her

and her sweetness amazes all

for how much ease she carries within herself

oh! and the part of her

that's savory

I'm yet to explore

I crave it all day

but the salt from her lips

is what I carry in my veins and into my heart

YOUR VOICE SOUNDS LIKE MY FATE

It's not the sound of your voice

but my fate

which I just heard

It's not your words

but the predictions of my life

you just uttered

MELODIOUS PROMISES

I forgot the old tunes

and lost all the rhythm

from the moment you walked into my life

with your melodious promises

OUR LOVE LIVED

Older than the first echo of the universe

and younger than this moment that I blinked

eternity ceased to exist

and our love lived

OWN THAT BROKEN PIECE

I didn't sew my broken pieces back into place

I got them embroidered

and turned them into vivid designs

which people admire and

look for ways to own

YOUR ARMS

Your arms are but the extensions of my sky which I always feared to have had fallen short of

NO BETTER WAY

I have told you

in every possible way

in every language known

in every emotion felt

just how much you matter to me

and how much I love you

but every time I do

I feel there could possibly be

a better way of doing it

NEED YOU BADLY

You are the song

I play on

gloomy days

you are the lamp

I light

on the darkest lone nights

you are the scent I wear

on old emerald embellished dresses

you are my sight

in my merry dreams

you are the tarnished coins

I collect

in my piggy bank

you are the air

I gasp for

after being left breathless

you are the love

I have always desired

so badly

LOVER's MASK

Can someone tell me

where they got their lover's masks

I only got the ones with smiles

THE LITTLE LIGHTHOUSE IN ME

I'm a lost ray of sunshine

wondering

why would I ever go back

to what burned me

and not be the little lighthouse

within myself

TINY FLAME

What to call that gush of wind

with which the tiny flame is in love

PAIN OR LIFE

you are synonymous to pain

but then you are to life too

ABSTRACT ACCENT

I had been carving my own self by shredding

shaving

stripping

peeling

and tearing off

my purity

to fit into this world

until I realised

I don't need to be a part of this jigsaw puzzle

but be my own kind of abstract accent

and stand out

FAKE REMEMBRANCES

The words you whispered

while you were caressing my hair

and pulled me closer

kissing my neck gently

have now become the things

which keep

pulsating and throbbing

rigorously and loudly

in my head

with repeated surrounding echoes

and choke my throat

with the irresistible fake remembrances

TEARS TASTE BETTER

From the evening

when the champagne was poured

for two

in newly bought flutes

to this moment

as I pour the whiskey

in the same old glass

tears started to taste better

like an aged wine

with each sip

bit by bit

we changed

FORGIVING SOUL

I'm the one

who keep forgiving

all his sins

but then

he is greater than me

he is a sinner

and he will keep repeating

until one fine day

I take it up a notch

to become superior

being a sinner is delightful

I will find

a forgiving soul

to continue ...

ARRESTED DREAMS

Few dreams were arrested

in her pretty eyes

she wished no escape

and loved to hide

but a milestone

in the memory lane

got her an undesired bail

dreams turned into tears

and got released

leaving an unsaid trail

HE IS EVERYTHING

An old library

therapeutic music

ancient ruins of

beautiful mysteries

He is everything

everything which I yearn

MY DARK CIRCLES

That night

long and dark

how it fell in love with my melancholia

and pleaded me

to keep it alive

in my proximities

and now my generous being

still carries it underneath my eyes

which they call dark circles

and all the nightmares

it lends oftentimes

are but my falling lashes

which they ask me to make wishes out of

to fulfill my due dreams

WOULD YOU LOVE ME

My mind is but the sky

would you fly

my heart is but a cage

would you stay

my body is but a temple

would you light a candle

my words are but a delusion

would you still fall for this confusion

ELIXIR OF LIFE

This city smells like

the elixir of life

the quintessential ether

the panaceas of absolute stillness

a sovereign remedy of life

with some tints of mirthful laughters

and few hints of inordinate pride

a little girl grew up dreaming here

SHORTCUT TO MY HEART

If I could ever make a map

of the words

of my poetry

perhaps you would know

the short cut to my heart

which you always have claimed

to be the longest distance

between us

KNOW HER

Some saw her in a crown

some saw her armored

some saw her naked

and some saw her covered in bandages

she sometimes sheds layers of lies

wearing all sorts of smiles

and adorns the attires of fury and passion

In every permutation and combination

you will find her beautiful and powerful

all at once

every time you meet her

TOO MUCH OF YOU

Too much of me

left you in confusion

while the Insufficiency of you

was a fair conclusion

DELAYED DREAM

You are my delayed dream

waiting for a merrier September night

MOST SENSE

He is the verse

making the most sense to me

in a library full of poetry

HE HAS A WAY

He has a way with words

you know

the accent of my acquainted language

the flair of perfection

his vivid charming chatter

touching my cordial dimensions

then again

he has a way with words

where his lips don't do anything

but meet mine

to tell me

he loves me

at my unholy

not so divine

I TRUSTED

My fault was that I asked if this road led somewhere

SHE IS A GODLY SCRIPTURE

She is art

a godly scripture

to tell you your purpose

not a beautiful decor accent

that you just admire

and forget

MAKE ME FAMOUS

Applause loudly for my poetry

and make me famous

let them judge the depths of my wounds

NUDE HUES

and all this time

in the nude hues of your memories

the drapes of my attire

tried to embrace my body

and all inches of it

just like you always tried

to fit perfectly

with the curves that I adorn

ALL MY BEING

When I tell you

I love you

I mean it with all my heart

and when I don't say it

I mean it with all my being

ACT OF LOVE

For some

it is sex

for some

it is making love

for some

it is the act of exquisite holiness

experiencing the utmost heavenly pleasure

by two age old souls

wanting to be one

getting lost with each other

and evolving like having found the existence

In the divine worlds of love

and that too in the presence of all the Gods

and one supreme being

such rare occasions are yet to be nomenclatured

and be brought into consciousness

ANOTHER WORLD

There might be another world

where people know each other by their souls

where there is no hatred and no pain

they connect through love instead of losses and gains

DARK AND YOUNG

Some I read

some I heard

rest I want to taste

on my lips

and on the tip of my tongue

all those poems you wrote for me

when your nights were dark and young

POSH DATE

One fine day

we plan to date

no exotic place

no fancy remake

just you and me

and your motor bike

from early evening

till late night

we keep on riding

talking loud

laughing high

munching nuts and chocopies

and as we part

memories framed in our hearts

and from then

we know breeze and speed

with a new name

half yours

and half mine

the most posh date ever

let it be in our hearts as headlines

THE TOY

I wrote *sun*

and the *stars*

I wrote *drugs*

and also *wars*

deep dark *oceans*

garlands and *flowers*

but I made a mistake

to not have written *toy*

for a gentleman defines all of above

while you are like every other boy

THE CUSP

Beneath

her

lashes

a

dream

crashes

every

midnight

as

she

fights

the

cusp

of

yesterday's

and

tomorrow's

plights

FREE MEALS

Some of us

are just

a free meal to

curious brains

lustful eyes

and

hungry egos

know your worth

and become good appetizers

to the ones

who value you

like a feast

from paradise

THE REAL STORY

Visitors

appreciate

the beauty

of the mosaic art

but he knows

the story

behind every piece

of her heart

NO WARS PLEASE

Some ugly days

scared my heart's core

and ruptured my naive soul

and all I want now

is to gather them all

revengefully

drawing from my memories

and blending to consistency

erasing all natural instincts

in a fine sparkling wine

I will pour them into a bottle

wouldn't mind not having corks

and gulp it down to my belly

twisting

twirling and grooving to its beats

and celebrate

the pains

and the triumphant scars

for I never had

and never will

believe in wars

JINXED BUT ADMIRED

The night still remained

while the clocks got tired

the moon ran out of stories

and the sun got fired

such was their love

one in the universe

Partly jinxed

Partly admired

VAULT OF YOUR HEART

A heart of gold

a heart of steel

a heart of stardust

my heart is of something

inexpensive and ordinary

nothing like the ones above

it is brittle and has no strength

yet can be used as gun powder

it is as transparent as the air

purest of all and everything fair

it has no weight

but can carry all of the mass

that you acquire in space

it is a heart

made up of glass

now

it's up to you

to play with it carelessly

or

to keep protected

in the vault of your

own heart

SHE IS UNFIT

She is the abundance of art

in this aesthetically scarce world

REFUSED PRAYERS

Those who refused her prayers now fondly read her
poetry

NEW ADRESS

Send your somber smiles

to the new address

for her vivaciously wrecked heart

is the perfect place to mourn

it gladly allows the solemn sorrows

freeing the vivid glories

bestowing bliss

SHE IS HERSELF

She is best at being herself

so she is best at being anything

ALL OF ME

Don't fall in love with me

fall for my poetry

all I can give you is poetry

and

my poetry can give you

all of me

A LITTLE TOO MUCH

And sometimes

silence becomes

a little too silent

and poetry becomes

a little too poetic

for few to understand

NO MORE WRITING

The time has come for me

to choose between

my happiness and

the readers' pleasure

because

if you start loving me again

I won't be writing anymore

I AM HEALING

I changed the disclaimer labels

of my habits

from injurious to healthy

like once

with each tear that I cried

I died

remembering you

and now

with each puff of a cigarette

I'm healing

forgetting you

AT ZERO

Between knowing my limits

and having no limits

I swung like a pendulum

with every to and fro

I lost magnitude

and gained momentum

sometimes I rested at zero

and sometimes got vivacious

sombrely acting astound

but mostly into a slumber

UNFAIR MIRROR

The mirror had been unfair to me

all those years

until one day I made friends with the camera

the camera has filters

unlike mirrors

HE WAS MY GOD

He

who was my god

has changed the rules of

one heart-one love

SCRIBBLE LOVE

The laced top

slipped down her shoulder

as he touched

the silk on her skin

with a deep sigh

closing her eyes

she prompted him

to scribble love

on each following inch of her body

with his lips

like a perfectly written manuscript

by two untutored artists

EVERYTHING BELONGS TO ME

While laying on silvery sand

the dying sun kissing my belly

glaring upon passionate waves

touching my soaked feet

desperate to embrace me

losing the ancient rhythm and pace

my mind fleeted away

prevailing alien thoughts

out of my drunken being

breaking up the present knots

oceans are nothing but tears

departing all pain and fears

some loyal heart had cried

the immortal love became glorious pearls

enchanting the content of salt

making sure no one taste the curse

and as they crash upon me

they might have recognised

the sun

the waves

the oceans

also those caves

and each present gaze

belongs to me

to my soul

timeworn yet pristine

CURSED POETRY

Neither does her poetry love her

nor does she love it

this is her disowned wrecked heart

which bleeds ink and verses

for lovers it may be a bliss

but for her it's nothing but a curse

YOUR LIES

It was terribly beautiful

to know that

all the truths in your heart

weren't sufficient to get to me

but your lies

I was unapproachable yet

so desirable to you

that I fell for your sweet nothings

and not for you

and now that I have unveiled all of it

how bad I wish

I hadn't

YOUR ABSENCE

A few pretty days

I love caressing your hair

with my fingers

while whispering love words in your ears

the rest of the prettier days

I love caressing the empty sheets of paper

with inks in my favourite colours

your presence is lovely

your absence has much more to love

MAKE LOVE TO SUSTAIN

Make love

like you do your best to sustain

It has to taste like food for the hungry

A LITTLE SLOW

Oh dear life

can you course a little slower

there are tasks that I left incomplete

there is some gratitude left to be felt

and a few heartfelt apologies

to the ones I ever hurt

Some riddles I left unsolved

my search for answers

I keep asking for

more smiles on some faces

I keep looking for

some dreams to be lived

some promises to be made

and then some more time

to keep those promises

as I try to match my pace

and go with your flow

please be lenient

and course a little slow

BEFRIENDED ME

The loneliness I once was afraid of

has befriended me dearly

ARE WE FREE

Flowing waters

chirping birds

and blowing breeze

are free to go any where

human brains are captives in their own thoughts

prevailing a greater thought

we are free

CAN I BORROW

Can I borrow some of your light please

this darkness scares me sometimes

can you hold my hands firmly

through my journey for a while

I want to feel safe and sound

maybe just for a mile

WELCOME HOME

She is the work of art

created by destiny and some wrong choices

her heart is a museum of moments kept safe

the creased eyes hold the history of a heartbreak

a failed love story but a victorious survival

the fallen tears telling unspoken tales

trembling feet standing tall

empty hands offer fulfilling love

there is so much yet to be visited

there is a lot yet to be explored

people admire the brightest parts

but a few know that beauty exists in the darkest yards

untouched

untold

unfelt

unfollowed

yet unfortunate

the doorstep is dusty with her trashed past

and still reads *welcome home*

such is she

a masterpiece

with darker blood n fewer bones

SHE CAN FORGIVE

She can forgive

but cannot forget

how he broke her heart

She spent ages at the airport

and he was busy

painting his raft

MOURNING UNIVERSE

Everything that felt abused and betrayed is now mourning our love

for e.g. the universe

PARTING WAYS

Pain had an amazing way

to introduce itself

It was waiting for love and loyalty

to part ways

REBELLIOUS TEAR

The trail of tears

kept watering

the dead hopes

till the last drop

became a rebel

and turned

into a dream

which now

lives in her pupil

and sees the world

like it was never

as bad a world

that could butcher her

PETTY SOULS

I slide away the pale curtains of my window
dawn today
has brought me a whole new canvas
which once was the surreal sky

my walking spirit took me to the bleakest spotlight
where I was amongst all the fairies in monochrome
waiting to be coloured with the pallet of the rainbow
how do I make them believe
that I'm no painter but an artist's spirit
who knows drama and can tiptoe
some salsa and ballet
but for all that I need my pointes
made of grains of drugs
and some fairy lights

whilst all that non vocal yet pursuant conversation

dusk barged in with my favourite packets of drugs

In a polaroid reel

the movie kept playing in my imagination

and the psychedelic *not so haunted*

imagination was the beatitude of those petty souls

NO MATTER WHAT

We shared a hundred goodbyes

and still returned

we broke every promise

and made better ones

we cursed each other

and kept sending wishes in tons

love is not all about

non failing commitments

It is about staying together

no matter what

REACHING OUT TO YOU

The sunset sky looks like

the colorful drapes of me

trying to reach out to you

where

I assume

your arms crave

to embrace me too

and as soon the moon shows up

with the troop of stars to tease me more

I do nothing

but write down

everything I feel

in your absence

MY HUMAN DIARY

You are my human diary
with the features to revert and advocate
keeping records of my sighs and sorrows
always handy
when I need to hush or whisper
or just need to enter
the score to my enigmatic smiles

you are like the colour gray
that knows how to absorb mishmash
and are aware of the ugly parts in me
can't ever have enough
you conceal
what pinks and purples have spoilt

you are my umbrella

weary yet warm

I keep in my handbag

for days

I would love to get drenched and dance

like life has taught me to

you are my ivory porcelain

with a tint of gold and hint of steel alloys

I use to fill in the cracks of my heart

to decorate

and to give strength

to endure further pressures

you are not a crush

neither are you the one

that I crave

you don't owe me kisses and cuddles

you are just a person next door

that I look up to

like an atlas or a thesaurus

you are the one I want by my side

when I feel week on my knees

and hold me up

with the glittering eyes and saying

don't you fear falling I'm here for you

you are the ascertain element of life

I somehow discovered

more important than the other five known to man

through which I thrive

no matter how tough it gets to imbibe

you would never hear me say

I love you

for there are no phrases

or even a library

that could describe

how a heart carries so much affinity

worth more than millions

AN ADDICTIVE GAME

You left me like an

addictive game

you can't master enough

each time you play

MYTHS OF LOVE

Last night

I was almost sober

when I was about to take

the first sip

from my whisky glass

and I was scrolling through

your old messages

thinking

how bad it felt

when every time I begged

for you to stay

a little longer

you packed

and left anyway

the lonesomeness fetched me

retardant thoughts

and I wondered how

the partially hidden faces

of you

and the partially revealed truths

of us

had become the only reason of survival between us

yet I kept forgetting all

and you carried the tradition

till I had had enough

blame my laughter

bursting spontaneity

or insane wit

that I carelessly dropped the glass

which was yet to be stained red

by my lips

and broke it

and I can't help but mock it God!

laying on the floor

it looked like

the half moon

timidly hiding itself

in the lap of the dark mysterious night

I laughed harder

and honestly

I was sober and liberated

letting the vivid side of the truths

sink in me

it was not a glass

that had just broke

but the *myth of love*

NO MORE DROWNING

My dreams

long lost in tears

will always make their way to

the shore

for the dark drowning waters

have become

buoyant lately

HIS TRANSPARENCY

My troubles were

all shades of dark

and the goodbyes were

odorless

and he walked in

with a handful of incense

with the ease of transparency

in his eyes

A DREAM LONG LIVED

I picked him from my favorite fairytale
when granny's books were all exhausted
I stuck to this one hero

his name I'm forgetting
I met him several times
he used to read me poems
and take me to lavenders fields
where we would sit by the old well
and talk and laugh for hours
we would eat berries and sing songs
days went by
until one fine morning
when I woke up
and everything was changed

my slippers and tops won't fit me anymore

my hair was long and skin was pink hued

I spoke softly and walked gently

blushing often and dreaming a lot

he was but a dream

well lived

in my best memories

he still lives

or somewhere with someone else

with some naive little heart

TOGETHER YET AFAR

We met like

two prisoners

sentenced for lifetime

kept in adjacent cells

across bars

together yet afar

BETWEEN THE KISSES

The

time

that

stopped

between

our

kisses

was

the

time

I lived

the most

DO NOT CALL ME A ROSE

the dark corner here

is full of moisture

and dust

also that window

seems too far

for the sunlight

to reach through

your love

is way too much

for me

when you called me a rose

and planted me

in apprehension of owning a fragrant garden

all I want

is for you

to stop

drowning me

in the water

that you pour

you think

is your love

HEADS OR TALES

let's decide the fate of this dreary night

let's toss with the

mascot of darkness

the face of moon

I kiss you

the rear of it

you kiss me

HUNGRY HEART

My heart

is hungry

to feed someone

with love

but

everyone else

is already

full of crap

LEAKED LOVE

Poor girl!

what are you seeking

a shoulder to lean on

a hand to hold you

some good ears

or your mother's lap

did you forget

you lost all

and the love you seek

has already leaked

did you forget

you are not allowed to complain

all you are supposed to do is

wear the perfect hostess's smile

even when you are unable to hold your broken pieces together

you still are not allowed to cry

because you have a heart

which maybe broken

but it's aura is to bless others

even if you are cursed

remind yourself well

get up and start again

and behave like nothing happened

HER OPTIONS

She waited for him like

a bee waits for flowers to bloom

or saplings wait for the sky to pour

soon she realised

she had options

unlike them

TINY ROSE

I was sitting on garden bench

sad

a tiny rose

in a thorny bush

whispered

Pluck me! if I can make you happy

YES! YOU LOVE ME TOO

I think

everest

you think

below your head

I feel

lava

you feel

frozen dead

I love you

you love me too

but

volatile

shallow

and withered

SIMPLY DISASTER

From colorless to red and then blue

transitions of pain occurred

from tears to blood and then inks

all I jotted on papers

call it aching love

ugly strokes of destiny

or simply disaster

LOST WORDS

The heart of the crumbled paper

had lost some words

later found stuck

on her drapes

the silks of which

often embrace her curves

and the tussled pearls

kiss her skin

like he never dreamed of

DONT SAY MY NAME

make sure you don't say my name

while you stab me

I have a habit to turn

smiling

every time I hear your voice

all while it would be tough for you

to face me

for my smile killed you so many times

and now this is you to return

FEELING FULL

I'm comfortably undeniably feeling full

unlike the emptiness

prior your presence

had lended

the numbing hollowed voids

it feels more like

free falling

or

falling in love

NO RESCUE BOATS FOR ME

Let me blame that heartbeat

mistakenly skipped

tried hard not to

when your lips touched

below the collar of my shirt

making the moments weaker

and created a whole new havoc of storms

between us

and I denied the rescue boats

ever after

FLOWERS OF HELL

The sweet seduction of your kisses

wild passion

more of a teaser

Is it the venom

of a traitorous serpent

or the nectar

of the flower

found in hell

DESTINY OF BOOK

She was like the destiny

of that book

kept in the library

dusty and webbed

in the corner shelf of the unvisited aisle

waiting to be chosen

but out of reach

of someone

who could admire

each word and each phrase

perfectly

rightly

for the forbidden books

with forgotten tales

are the best treasures

to be admired and availed

UNSUNG SONGS

The songs I wanted you to sing for me

are often heard

on my terrace

hummed languidly

perhaps the moonstruck nightingale

mourns over the incomplete love story

I wonder

how bad it would have been for you

missing me

in those lonely evenings

sitting on the same bench in the park

when we admired the world

perhaps more than each other

and that poor bird in the shrubs

is the sole witness of our last hug

the songs now are left unsung

and the nature unvisited

except that bird which still follows

this ritual religiously

NOT MY BAGGAGE

In the journey of my life

where I find only

parching drought in the world

here I'm searching

that generous tree

under the cool shade of which

I can relieve

some of the baggage

from the aching shoulders

of my exhausted soul

carrying since forever

which doesn't even belong to me

I AM HIS PART

and

that moment

I felt

I'm just a worthless drop in a river

running hopelessly

for my existence doesn't make any difference

and the next moment

my phone rang

and his voice

to me

felt like the ocean of love

ready to embrace that river and

guarding my chaos with it's calm

that mighty moment

in the weakest thought

had given me hopes

and gaiety it brought

and

I'm happy

I'm his part

though miles apart

but

I reside in him

I always have

I always will

LOSING YET WINNING

Let me tell you

how fond I am

of dialogues and debate sessions

and proving my point

till I win

but seriously

with you

I just love

losing all I have

by not uttering a word

but letting the sounds of my heartbeats

break the rhythms of silence

and mystic gestures of eyes

convey

what my heart wishes and desires

CHURCH BELLS

because your love was constantly confusing her

between coffee table greetings

and evening bar compliments and

all she ever expected from you

was not the echoing sweet nothings

but to have her heart heard

which beats much like

church bells

COUNTING SHEEPS

and every night

the last sheep I count

loses the herd

because your memories

take a hold of my mind

so strong

when I counted it's predecessors

WILL YOU DISAPPEAR

Drinks after drinks

I thought you will disappear

from my thoughts

but now

you smile in front of my eyes

and that too

in a grid of four

YOUR PRINTS

You may not exist in the blue print of my life line

but my heart has enough fingerprints

and footprints

of yours

for me to claim from destiny

that how often you have had the privilege

of touching it

and staying here well accorded

OUR INCOMPLETE STORY

while turning the pale pages

I stopped at the sight

of an old dried flower

I touched gently the petals

closing my wistful eyes

and after a while

I realized

the story I just switched to

is also the one

which was left incomplete

MORE THAN BLESSED

She is not blessed

She is a blessing

MY COPING MECHANISM

When u keep on blaming me

and I see no other mechanism

to cope up

with that humiliation

but to laugh abruptly

how people then decide

to end their lives

has a lot to do

with when that mechanism ceases to work

YOUR NAME

What noise would my heart make if it pronounced your name like everyone else does

EXPIRED APOLOGIES

now these expired apologies can only embellish my scars

MY HEART AND MIND

Sometimes it's my mind

which keeps on hushing

all the queries

my heart puts forward

and sometimes it's my heart

which consoles

the mind

for all it's losses

WHO IS THE LUCKY ONE

They ask me

while they read

who is the lucky one

well! poetry doesn't serve much to realists

there doesn't exist a man of my dreams

and I write

about love

rationally nonexistent

LIFE LESSONS

Very gently

my heart asked me today

when will you start learning lessons

letting me heal in peace

ABOUT AUTHOR

Shilpa Panigrahi was born on April 15, 1977 in New Delhi and lives with her husband, daughter, son and her niece in Faridabad, India.

Graduated from Delhi university and having a degree in Bachelor of Education, she chose to be a homemaker.

This being her debut book, she has greater plans on writing more in the future.

Instagram
@shilpa_panigrahi15
Facebook
@asmiarth
Twitter
@panigrahishilpa